CRANES

by Kathryn Clay

CAPSTONE PRESS
a capstone imprint

Little Pebble is published by Capstone Press,
1710 Roe Crest Drive, North Mankato, Minnesota 56003
www.mycapstone.com

Library of Congress Cataloging-in-Publication Data
Names: Clay, Kathryn, author.
Title: Cranes / by Kathryn Clay.
Description: North Mankato, Minnesota : Capstone Press, [2017] |
Series: Little pebble. Construction vehicles at work | Audience: Ages 4–8. |
Audience: K to grade 3. | Includes bibliographical references and index.
Identifiers: LCCN 2015048723| ISBN 9781515725282 (library binding) |
ISBN 9781515725336 (pbk.) | ISBN 9781515725381 (ebook pdf)
Subjects: LCSH: Cranes, derricks, etc.—Juvenile literature. |
Hoisting machinery—Juvenile literature.
Classification: LCC TJ1363 .C57 2017 | DDC 621.8/73—dc23
LC record available at http://lccn.loc.gov/2015048723

Editorial Credits
Erika L. Shores, editor; Juliette Peters and Kayla Rossow, designers;
Eric Gohl, media researcher; Tori Abraham, production specialist

Photo Credits
Alamy: Cultura Creative, 17, Ivan Vdovin, 5, Radharc Images, 21, Tetra Images, 11;
iStockphoto: HHakim, 7; Shutterstock: Alexandr Shevchenko, 1, bogdanhoda, 19,
Deviatov Aleksei, 15, Dmitry Kalinovsky, 9, Rihardzz, 13, Vadim Ratnikov, 10,
Zorandim, cover

Design elements: Shutterstock

Printed in the United States of America.
112016   010160R

Table of Contents

About Cranes

Look up high!

It's a tall crane.

Cranes lift.

Their loads go

high up in the air.

See the long arm?

It is called a boom.

boom

9

Here is a hook.

It picks up big blocks.

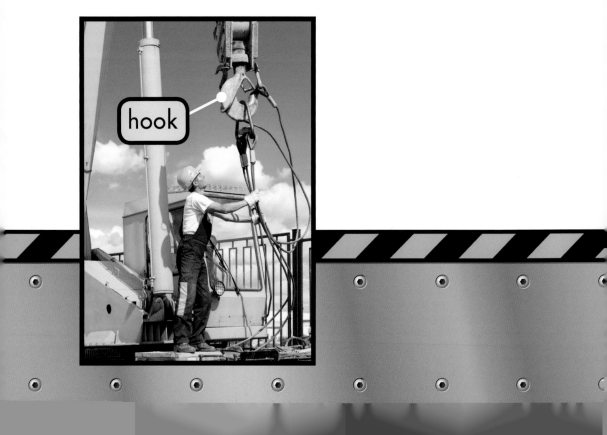

Here is a bucket.

It scoops sand.

bucket

This crane has tracks.
They go over mud
and rocks.

track

15

At Work

A crane lifts beams.

Beams are made of steel.

The workers need

heavy tools.

A crane carries them.

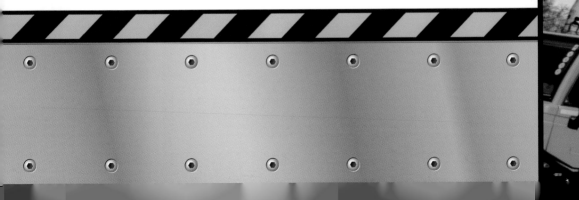

Here is the new building.

Nice job, crane!

Glossary

boom—the long metal arm of a crane

load—the thing a crane lifts

steel—a hard, strong metal

track—a metal belt that runs around wheels

Read More

Askew, Amanda. *Cranes.* Mighty Machines. Buffalo, N.Y.: Firefly Books, 2010.

Hayes, Amy. *Big Cranes.* Machines that Work. New York: Cavendish Square Publishing, 2016.

Lennie, Charles. *Cranes.* Construction Machines. Minneapolis: Abdo Kids, 2015.

Internet Sites

FactHound offers a safe, fun way to find Internet sites related to this book. All of the sites on FactHound have been researched by our staff.

Here's all you do:
Visit *www.facthound.com*
Type in this code: 9781515725282

Check out projects, games and lots more at
www.capstonekids.com

Index